273303

MEDICAL EXAMINATION

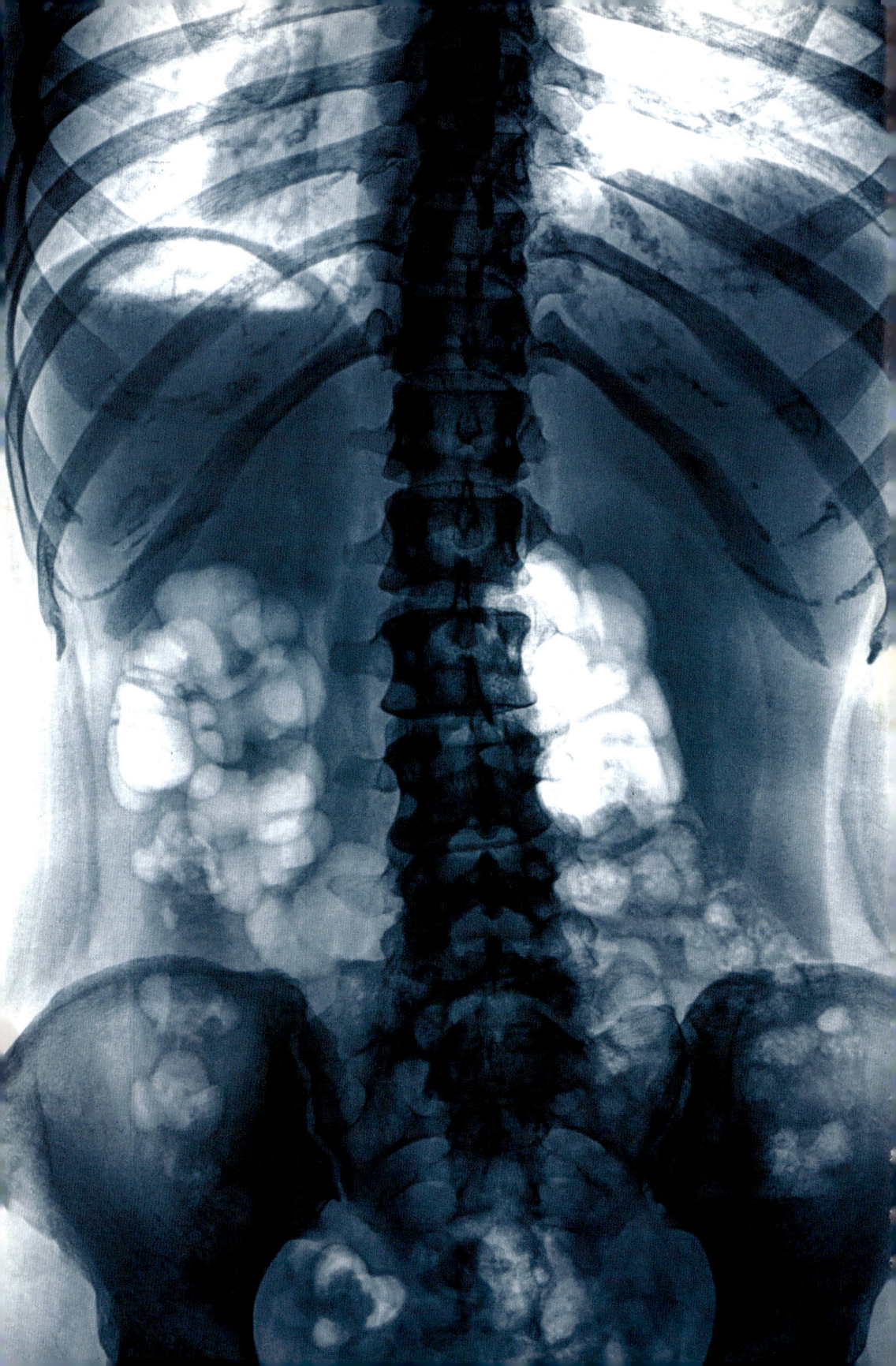

MEDICAL EXAMINATION
ODYSSEYS

VALERIE BODDEN

CREATIVE EDUCATION · CREATIVE PAPERBACKS

Published by Creative Education and Creative Paperbacks
P.O. Box 227, Mankato, Minnesota 56002
Creative Education and Creative Paperbacks
are imprints of The Creative Company
www.thecreativecompany.us

Design by Blue Design (www.bluedes.com)
Production by Joe Kahnke
Art direction by Rita Marshall
Printed in China

Photographs by Alamy (Sergio Azenha, B Christopher, Collection Christophel, dpa picture alliance, imageBROKER, XiXinXing, ZUMA Press Inc.), Creative Commons Wikimedia (Nevit Dilmen; LASZLO ILYES/The Feast; National Institutes of Health, Health & Human Services/ U.S. Government; Rembrandt/The Yorck Project/Royal Picture Gallery Mauritshuis; Andries Stock/Wellcome Images/Wellcome Library), Getty Images (Hulton Archive/Stringer), iStockphoto (Rich Legg, spxChrome, Steve Turner), Mary Evans Picture Library (Ronald Grant Archive/Mary Evans/CBS/JERRY BRUCKHEIMER TELEVISION/TOUCHSTONE TELEVISION), Newscom (HANDOUT/KRT, Zuma), Science Source (Peter Menzel), Shutterstock (AkeSak, thailoei92)

Copyright © 2018 Creative Education, Creative Paperbacks
International copyright reserved in all countries. No part of this book may be reproduced in any form without written permission from the publisher.

Library of Congress Cataloging-in-Publication Data
Names: Bodden, Valerie, author.
Title: Medical examination / Valerie Bodden.
Series: Odysseys in crime scene science.
Includes bibliographical references and index.
Summary: An in-depth look at how medical examiners, pathologists, and other forensic professionals examine and identify victims to help solve crimes, employing real-life examples such as genocide cases.

Identifiers: LCCN 2015027749 / ISBN 978-1-60818-683-9 (hardcover) / ISBN 978-1-62832-472-3 (pbk) / ISBN 978-1-56660-719-3 (eBook)

Subjects: LCSH: 1. Forensic pathology—Juvenile literature.
2. Forensic biology—Juvenile literature. 3. Criminal investigation—Juvenile literature. 4. Evidence, Criminal—Juvenile literature. 5. Forensic sciences—Juvenile literature.
6. Medical examiners (Law)—Juvenile literature.
Classification: LCC RA1063.4.B63 2016 / DDC 363.25/62—dc23

CCSS: RI 8.1, 2, 3, 4, 5, 8, 10; RI 9-10.1, 2, 3, 4, 5, 8, 10; RI 11-12.1, 2, 3, 4, 5, 10; RST 6-8.1, 2, 5, 6, 10; RST 9-10.1, 2, 5, 6, 10; RST 11-12.1, 2, 5, 6, 10

First Edition HC 9 8 7 6 5 4 3 2 1
First Edition PBK 9 8 7 6 5 4 3 2 1

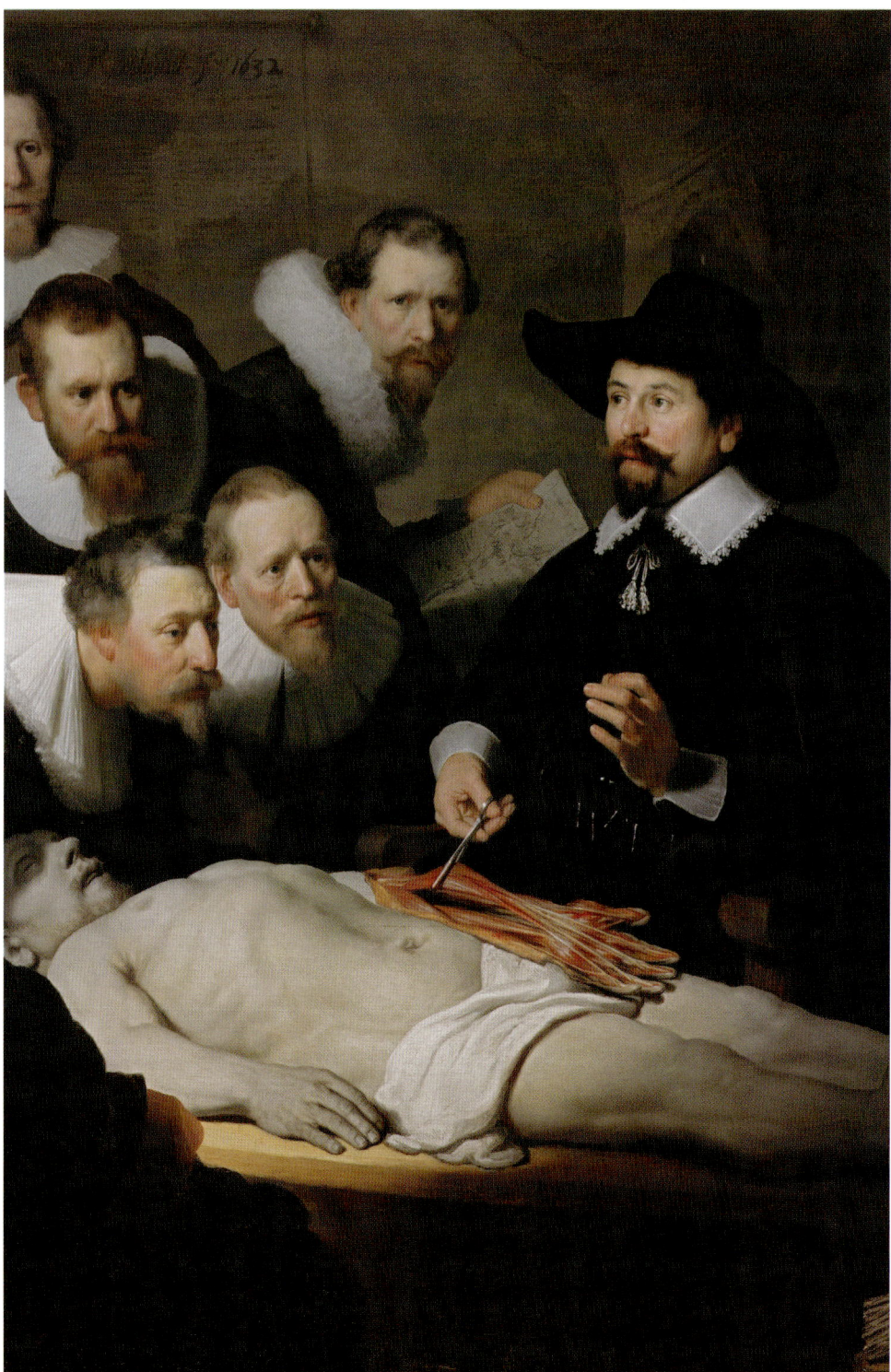

CONTENTS

Introduction **9**
Where There's a Body **11**
What the Bugs Can Tell 19
Letting the Dead Speak **25**
An Old Science 31
Skeleton Crew **38**
Righting Wrongs 44
Fictional Forensics **51**
The Body Farm 63
Last Chance **64**
You Be the Pathologist 67
Glossary **76**
Selected Bibliography **78**
Websites **79**
Index **80**

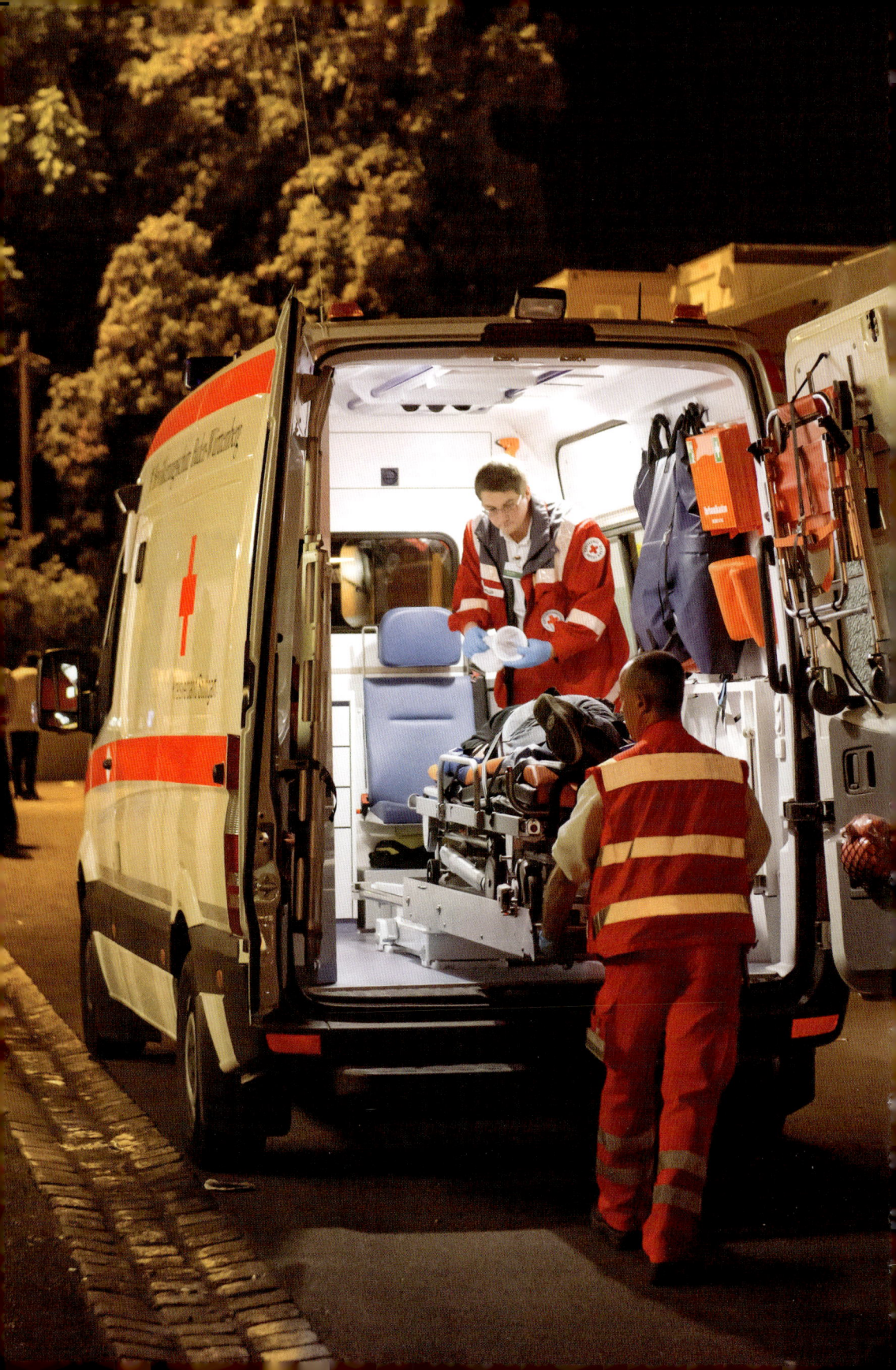

MEDICAL EXAMINATION

Introduction

Blue and red lights sweep across the front of a home. They reflect off jagged shards of glass in a broken first-floor window. Inside, books and pictures have been tossed to the floor. Papers hang from ransacked drawers. Two plates—their food still warm—sit on the kitchen table. A small red spot stains the floor under one of the chairs. This looks like a crime scene. But by the time police

OPPOSITE: Among the first responders to arrive at a crime scene are emergency medical technicians (EMTs). Their primary duty is to save lives and help anyone who is injured, even if it means they accidentally destroy some evidence at the scene in the process.

arrived, the house was empty. Now investigators must use crime scene science to help solve the mystery of what happened here—and who did it.

Crime scene science is also referred to as forensic science. Forensic science is simply science that is used to solve crimes and provide facts in a legal trial. Solving a crime often involves many forensic scientists, each specializing in a different area. When a crime involves a dead body, one of the first specialists called is the medical examiner. Other specialists, such as forensic anthropologists and forensic odontologists, may also work the case. For all of them, the goal is the same: identify the victim and determine what happened to him or her. Doing so can be the key to solving the case.

MEDICAL EXAMINATION

Where There's a Body

When someone dies in a hospital, the patient's doctor determines a cause of death and signs the death certificate. Only rarely is the person's body autopsied, or examined after death. And then, it is done only with the family's permission. Such autopsies are generally carried out for the purposes of medical research. Doctors might want to learn more about how a specific disease affects the body, for example.

But when someone dies violently or unexpectedly, without a doctor present, it generally requires further investigation. Such deaths are considered medicolegal cases. In other words, their investigation uses medical skills to determine whether a death occurred as the result of a crime.

In some counties of the United States, coroners are responsible for medicolegal cases. Coroners are elected government officials who do not necessarily have medical training. Many are also funeral directors or sheriffs. In other places, death investigations are handled by medical examiners. Medical examiners are appointed to their position. All medical examiners are physicians, and many are forensic pathologists. A forensic pathologist is a doctor trained in recognizing diseases and injuries that cause death. Some coroners and medical examiners have a staff of forensic pathologists who perform autopsies for them.

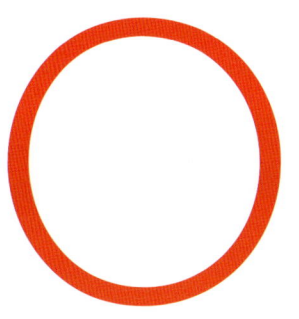Once a call comes in that a body has been discovered, the medical examiner or coroner goes to the crime scene. The body is now considered evidence, and no one may touch or move it without the medical examiner's consent. The first thing the medical examiner does is certify that the victim is, indeed, dead. This is an easy task if the body is decomposing. But if the victim appears to have died recently, the medical

OPPOSITE Using crime scene tape and other barricades, police officers set up a perimeter around a crime scene until investigators—including the medical examiner—are finished documenting the area and gathering evidence.

examiner must first check for signs of life. She looks for a pulse, heartbeat, or breathing. The medical examiner might also take stock of the scene to figure out if there are any clues as to the cause of death. She might examine medicines, dishes, or garbage cans for signs of drugs or the last food eaten, for example.

The medical examiner also looks for clues about the postmortem interval, or how long ago the person died. This helps her estimate the time of death. As soon as a person dies, certain changes begin occurring in the body. Because these changes are well-documented and predictable, they can be used to figure out how long someone has been dead.

After death, the body generally cools at a rate of 1.5 to 2.5 °F (0.9 to 1.4 °C) per hour. It cools at this rate for the first 12 hours. After that, it cools about 1 °F (0.6 °C)

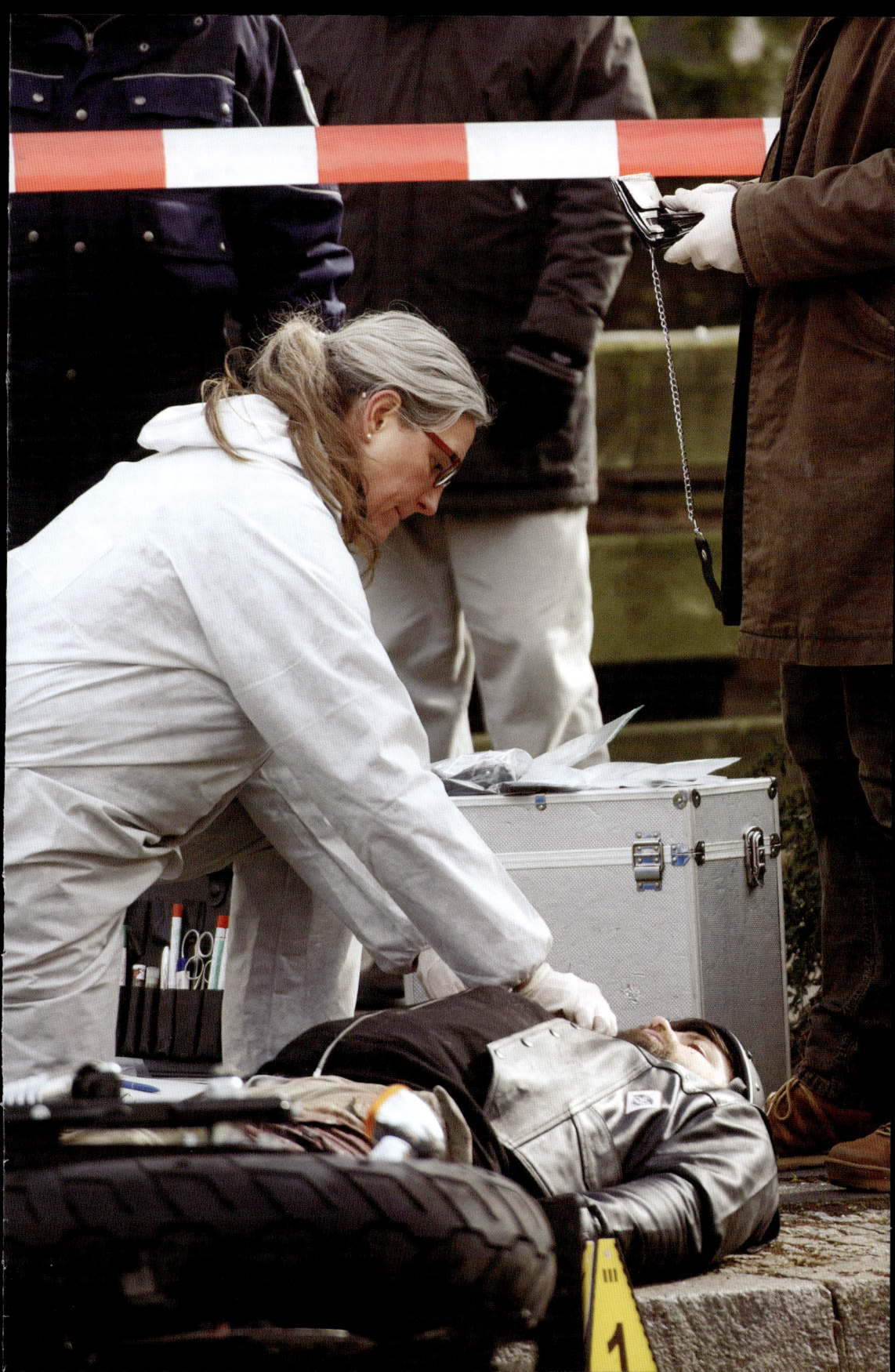

per hour. The cooling stops when the body reaches the temperature of its surroundings. This cooling is known as *algor mortis*. It can be used to estimate how long a body has been dead. But investigators have to take other conditions into account as well. If the air temperature is warmer than body temperature, for example, the body may actually get warmer after death. Bitterly cold temperatures may cause the body to cool more quickly than normal. Humidity, wind, and the victim's size and clothing can also affect cooling.

Another factor used to find time of death is *livor mortis*, also known as lividity. After the heart stops pumping, gravity pulls blood into the lowest parts of the body. The blood pools there, leaving reddish-purple marks on the skin. A body lying on its back, for example, would show lividity in the back, buttocks, and back of the legs. No marks are left wherever the body is pressed against a hard surface, such as the floor, though. Lividity starts to show up 30 to 60 minutes after death. By about three or four hours, it is fully developed. During this time, an investigator can press the colored area with his thumb, and it will blanch, or turn pale. By about 8 to 12 hours after death, however, the blood **coagulates**. The skin will no longer blanch if pressed. This is referred to as fixed lividity.

Medical examiners at the scene also look for signs of *rigor mortis*, or stiffening of the muscles. Immediately after death, the muscles become very loose. It takes between two and six hours for the muscles to begin to contract. This stiffening starts with small muscles such as the jaw. After about 12 hours, the entire body has stiffened. Rigor mortis generally remains for one to three days. Then it

> **TAKEAWAY**
>
> Algor, livor, and rigor mortis are useful for estimating a postmortem interval of up to several hours.

slowly releases as the body's tissues begin to break down.

Algor, livor, and rigor mortis are useful for estimating a postmortem interval of up to several hours. But if a body has been dead for days or weeks or years, the medical examiner may need to look at other signs. One way to tell how long a body has been dead is by looking at the amount of decomposition. Immediately after a person dies, the body begins to decay, inside and out. Internally, the body's cells fall apart. They release **enzymes** that break down tissues in a process known as autolysis. Externally, tissues are broken down by bacteria and microorganisms in a process known as putrefaction. Within 24 to 48 hours after death, the skin begins to take on a greenish color. Soon afterward, it swells from

What the Bugs Can Tell

Entomology is the study of insects. Forensic entomology is the study of insects in relation to dead bodies. Many insects are attracted to a rotting corpse. The first to arrive are usually blowflies. These generally reach the body about two days after death and lay eggs on it. When the larvae—called maggots—hatch, they begin to feed on the body. Entomologists have documented the blowfly life cycle. They know how long each stage takes under various environmental conditions. So they can use measurements of maggot development to figure out how long the body has been there. Different insect species are attracted to a corpse at different times. So entomologists can also examine the kinds of bugs present to help determine how long the person has been dead.

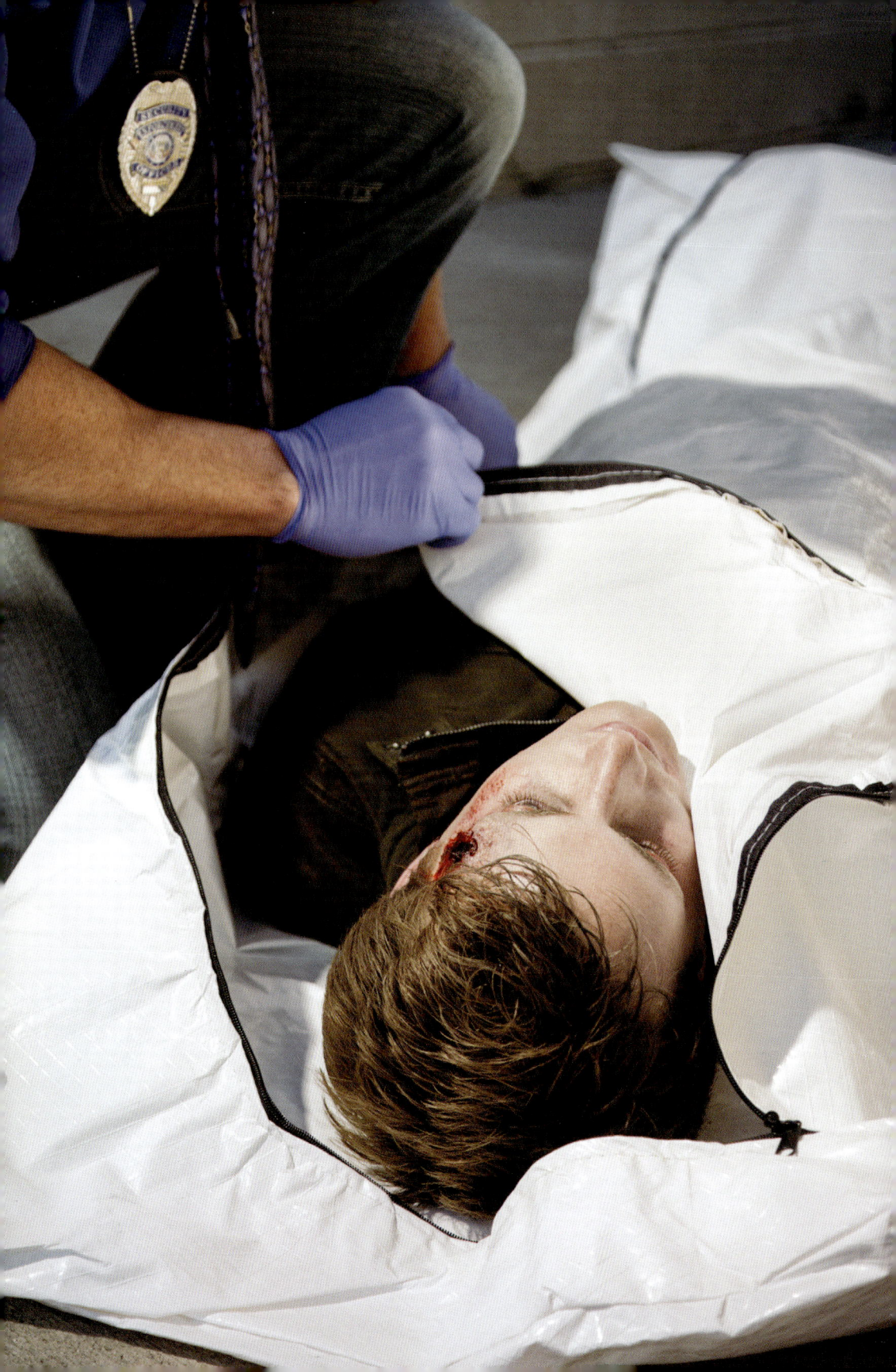

OPPOSITE Used to transport bodies to the morgue, body bags are made of heavy-duty, water-resistant materials such as plastic or tarpaulin, with a full-length zipper down the side.

gases released by bacteria. Later, the skin turns purple, brown, or black. The swelling collapses, and the body organs liquefy. The body continues to rot until only bones are left. How quickly this occurs depends on the temperature, environment, and other factors. A body left above ground can be skeletonized within two weeks in a hot climate. But a body buried in a shallow grave may retain some tissue for up to three years.

Once they have established a preliminary time of death, medical examiners oversee the body as it is placed into a body bag. From the crime scene, the body goes to the morgue. There, it is refrigerated to slow decomposition until an autopsy can be performed.

Despite the best efforts of American forensic pathologists, anthropologists, and odontologists, some 13,000 dead bodies remain unidentified. Some are kept in morgues, while others have been cremated or buried.

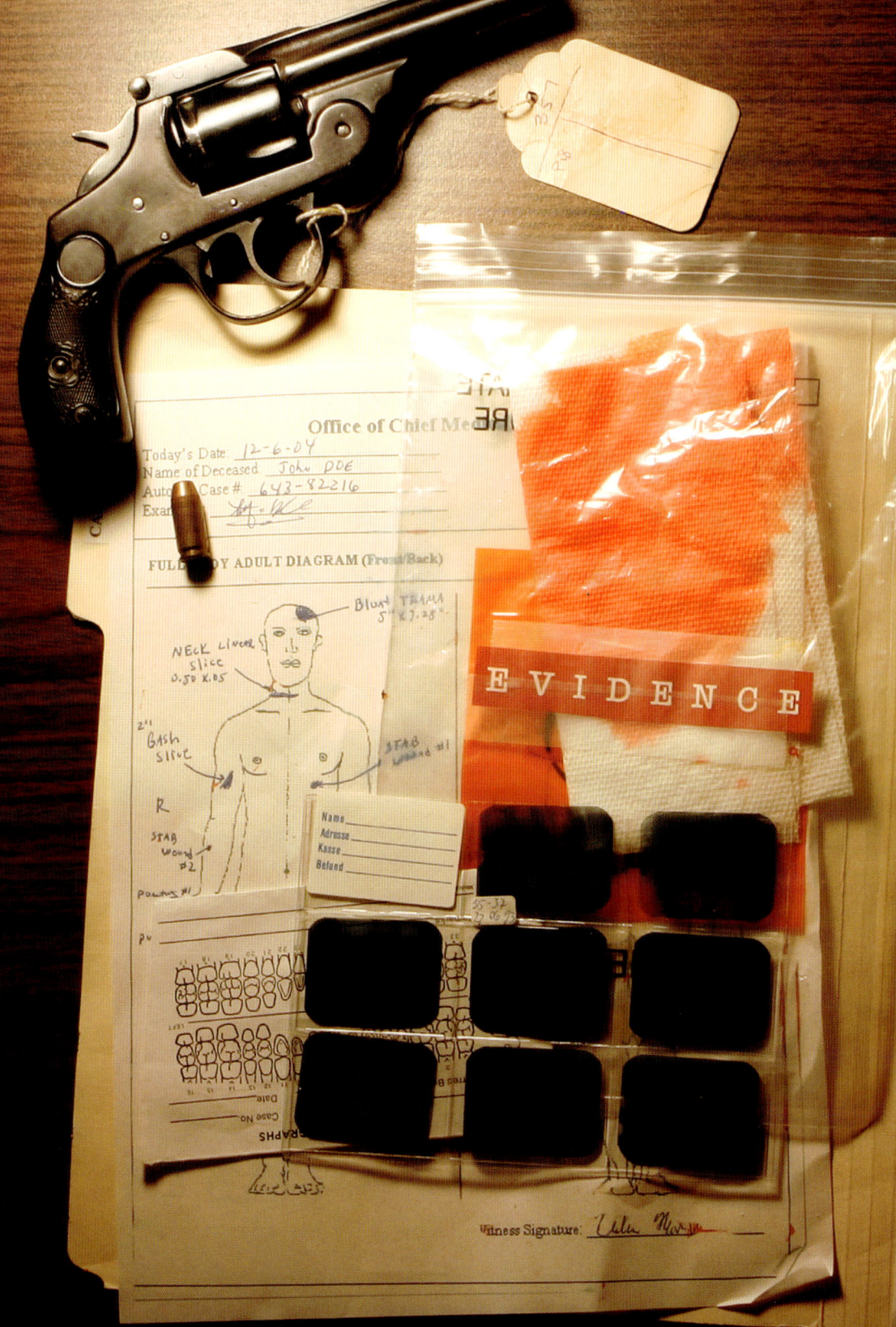

MEDICAL EXAMINATION

Letting the Dead Speak

The main purpose of an autopsy is to establish the cause, mechanism, and manner of death. The *cause* is the injury or disease that led to a person's death. A gunshot wound can be a cause of death. The *mechanism* describes the changes in the body that resulted from the cause of death. These are what prevented the victim's life from continuing. If the cause of death is a gunshot wound, the

OPPOSITE: Medical examiners must document every step of the autopsy. Detailed notes of their observations, scans, and diagrams help the examiner determine the cause, mechanism, and manner of death. Such documentation is also useful if a medical examiner must testify in a trial.

TAKEAWAY

"The concern in this room is not to bring the patient back to life; it is to speak with and for the dead."

mechanism of death might be bleeding in the chest cavity. The *manner* refers to how the cause of death occurred. There are only five manners of death: natural, accidental, suicide, homicide, or undetermined. Although the autopsy can help determine the manner of death, the circumstances surrounding the death also play a large part. In one case, a man was found dead in an empty swimming pool, his skull fractured. Investigators wondered if the man jumped or was pushed. But then they saw in a photograph that his shoe was untied. They concluded that the death was an accident. He had fallen into the pool after tripping over his shoelace.

Before beginning an autopsy, the pathologist puts on scrubs, a face mask, latex gloves, and booties that slip over the shoes. This gear provides a layer of protection against bloodborne **pathogens** such as HIV and hepatitis. It also guards against airborne pathogens such as pneumonia or **tuberculosis**.

The pathologist lays out his tools, which might seem surprisingly low-tech—and large. "To anyone accustomed to emergency room television shows, the utensils of the morgue are going to look big and urgent—more like hardware than surgical supply," said Michael Baden, former chief medical examiner for New York City. "But the concern in this room is not to bring the patient back to life; it is to speak with and for the dead. And that requires having a look and moving things around.... Lying

MEDICAL EXAMINATION

next to the scalpels are a bread knife, pruning clippers, and a vibrating bone saw." The bread knife is for cutting sections of organs. The saw cuts through the skull. And the clipper is used for the ribs. Other tools include a ruler, a scale, and microscopes.

The pathologist is rarely alone during an autopsy. An assistant helps with making cuts and measurements. In addition, crime-scene technicians, police photographers, and detectives often attend autopsies. They document the procedure and collect evidence found on the body.

Before the pathologist makes a single cut, the body is photographed both clothed and unclothed. It is also weighed and measured. Any defining characteristics—eye and hair color, tattoos, or scars—are photographed and recorded to aid in identifying the victim. The body may be X-rayed as well. This is especially useful if the

BELOW As forensic pathologists work, they wear protective gear, including gloves and masks, to protect themselves from possible diseases and to ensure that they do not introduce their own DNA into the sample they are withdrawing.

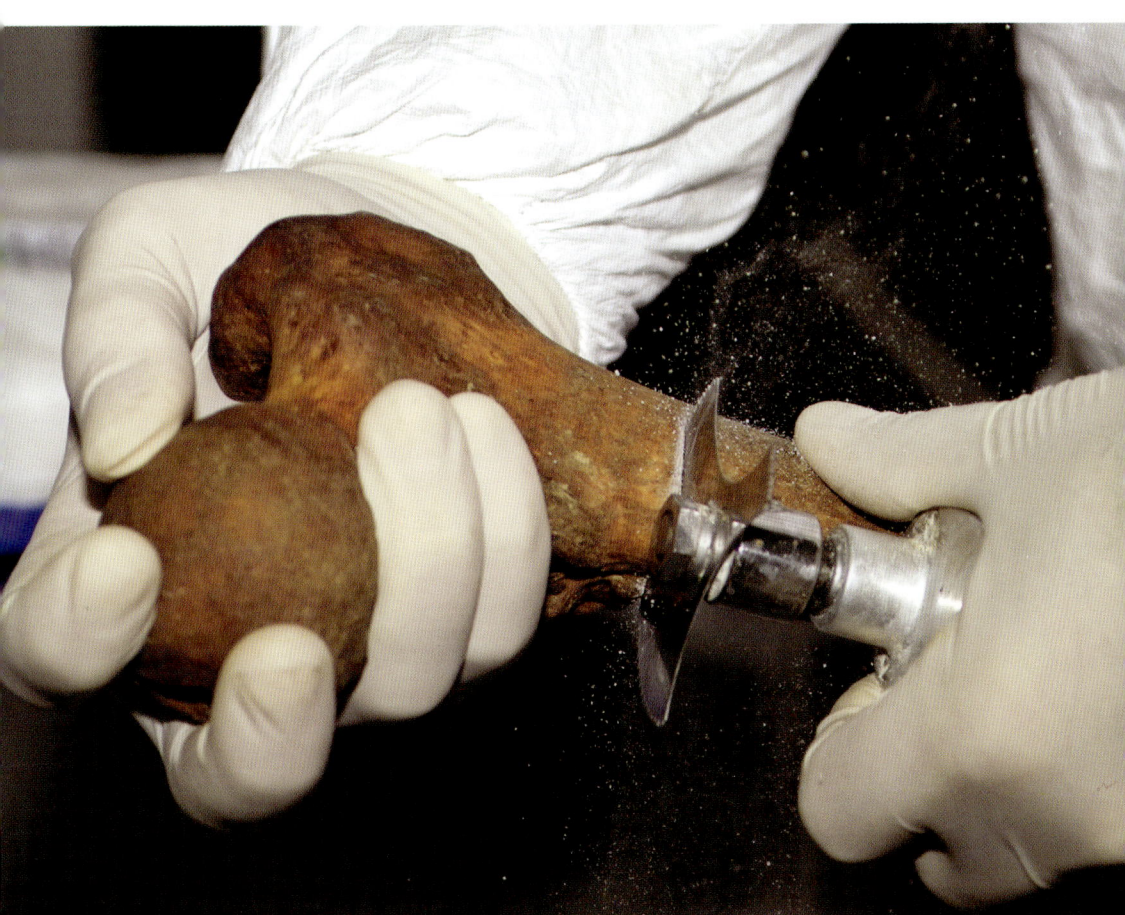

MEDICAL EXAMINATION

An Old Science

As early as the fifth century B.C., the Greeks performed autopsies on criminals and soldiers who died in war. In the first century B.C., the Roman physician Antistius examined Julius Caesar's 23 stab wounds to find the one that was fatal. In China, 13th-century physician Song Ci published a book urging medical examinations to determine cause of death. The book outlined how water in the lungs might indicate drowning, while bruising of the throat often meant strangulation. Meanwhile, autopsies were forbidden throughout much of Europe until the 1300s and 1400s. Then medical students were allowed to perform autopsies in a search for a cure to the **plague**. Modern autopsy procedures date to the 1850s and Rudolf Virchow's publication of *Cellular Pathology*. The book included guidelines on the microscopic examination of tissue.

pathologist needs to find the path a bullet took through the body.

The pathologist then performs a careful external examination. He takes note of any obvious signs of cause of death. Many forms of violent death—such as gunshots and stabbings—leave distinctive marks on the body. Marks circling the neck might point to strangulation. Bruises (also known as contusions) can imply the use of a blunt weapon. Tiny pinpricks of blood on the face can suggest smothering. During the external exam, **trace evidence** is collected from the body. This includes fingernail clippings, which might have traces of the attacker's **DNA** under them. The victim's fingerprints are also taken. Finally, the body is washed to prepare for the internal exam.

For the internal exam, the pathologist begins by making a Y-shaped cut from shoulder to shoulder and down the torso. The skin is pulled back from the cut. The ribs are also cut to allow access to the internal organs.

These organs—including the heart, lungs, stomach, and liver—are removed from the body. Each organ is weighed and examined. Small slices may be cut off each for further microscopic study. The pathologist also notes any damage caused to the organs, as by a knife wound. If the victim was shot, the pathologist must remove all bullet fragments as well. Usually, the internal exam reinforces what the pathologist already suspected from the external exam. Bruises outside the body are often joined by severe damage to the internal organs, for example. That was true in the case of Debra Barth, who was found under a pile of boxes in her basement. Bruises covered her body. The autopsy showed massive internal damage from a beating, including broken ribs and punctured lungs.

Other causes of death, such as drowning, asphyxiation, and hypothermia, leave almost no signs. In these cases,

OPPOSITE The U.S. National Library of Medicine features an exhibit called *Visible Proofs: Forensic Views of the Body* that explores the history of forensics. It includes sketches, writings, and even preserved organs, such as this heart of a 26-year-old man who was fatally shot in 1937. Organs were—and still are—frequently collected for teaching purposes.

pathologists have to make their determination by ruling out all other possible causes of death. They also have to consider environmental factors, including where the body was found. Poisoning, drug overdose, and alcohol also leave few obvious signs. To test for them, the pathologist collects blood, urine, **vitreous humor**, **bile**, and tissues to be sent for **toxicological** analysis. The contents of the stomach may be sent to the toxicology lab as well.

Once the torso exam is complete, the pathologist moves on to the head. He makes a cut from ear to ear over the head. Then he peels the skin forward and examines the skull for fractures or signs of bleeding or bruising. Using a saw, he cuts the skull open. The brain is removed and examined as well. When the autopsy is complete, small samples of all tissues are placed into jars. They are preserved with a chemical called formalin. Then the

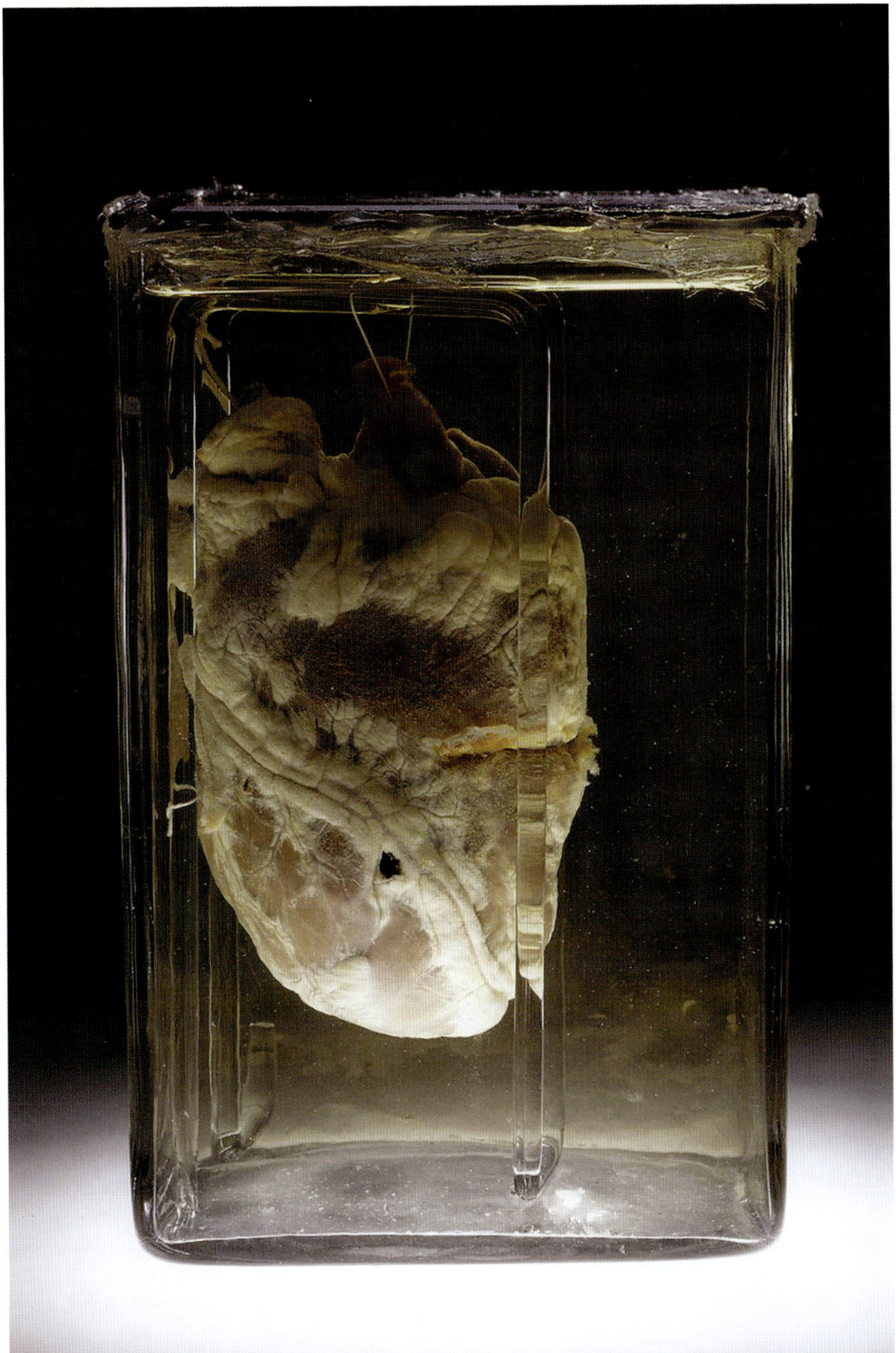

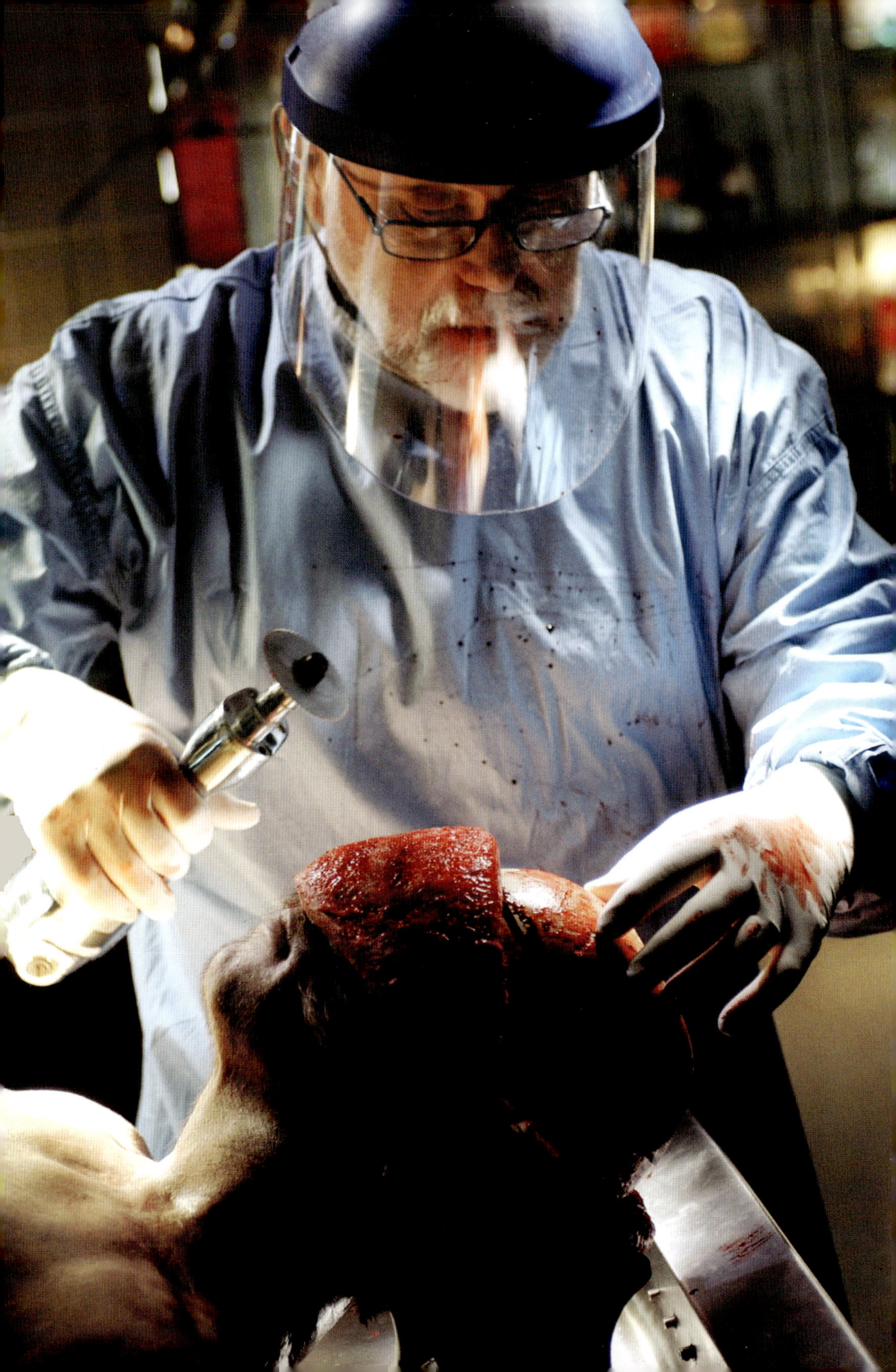

TAKEAWAY

Most autopsies take three to four hours to complete. Sometimes they take up to a full day, depending on the complexity of the case.

organs are returned to the body, and the skin is sutured back together.

Most autopsies take three to four hours to complete. Sometimes they take up to a full day, depending on the complexity of the case. Further testing, such as toxicological analysis, adds more time. As he works, the pathologist takes detailed notes, either on paper or into a voice recorder. After the autopsy is complete, he writes up a final report. This will be used in court in the case of criminal deaths.

MEDICAL EXAMINATION

MEDICAL EXAMINATION

Skeleton Crew

Sometimes, by the time a body is discovered, it is mostly decomposed. Or it may have been burned. Sometimes bodies are purposely destroyed by acid or other substances. In these cases, there often isn't enough tissue left for an autopsy. But bones are made of calcium and other dense minerals. They can survive for centuries after tissue has decayed. And, like tissues, bones can tell a story. The people called on to interpret that story are forensic anthropologists.

An anthropologist studies human culture and biology (called physical anthropology). Forensic anthropologists are experts in physical anthropology—particularly the skeletal system. They examine bones to help identify victims and determine how they died.

When decomposed human remains are found buried in an outdoor grave, a forensic anthropologist is often called to the scene. Before anyone begins digging, the anthropologist divides the site into a grid pattern. Each section of the grid is searched separately. Using hand trowels, dental picks, bamboo sticks, and paintbrushes, the soil is removed. Only about one or two inches (2.5–5.1 cm) are dug out at a time.

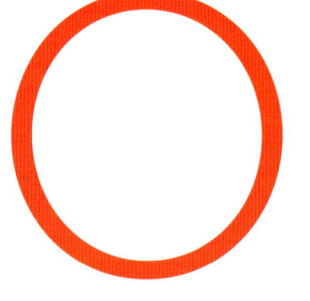

Once all parts of the skeleton have been unearthed, they are taken back to the lab for further analysis. The anthropologist begins with a thorough external examination. She then boils the skeleton to clean any flesh from it before assembling the bones in **anatomical** order. If the skull or other bones are fractured, they can be pieced back together with glue and wooden sticks.

Now the anthropologist can get down to her main task—identifying the remains. She starts by putting together a biological profile. This includes the person's age, sex, ancestry, and height. All of this information is learned from the skeleton.

Babies are born with more than 300 bones. But as they grow, these bones unite, or fuse together, in a specific order. The anthropologist examines which bones have

BELOW When only a victim's bones remain, scientists first attempt to identify the remains using anthropological methods. They may also employ pathological methods. Depending on the state of the decomposing body, identification can take weeks, months, or even years.

MEDICAL EXAMINATION

already united and which have not yet fused. This allows her to estimate a child or young adult's age. For victims over the age of about 28, anthropologists use other bone indicators to determine the age. They look for signs of degeneration, wear, and arthritis, for example.

Sex can be impossible to determine from the skeletal remains of children. But in adults, a female's pelvis is wider than a male's. In addition, a male's jaw tends to be more pronounced. So does the brow ridge (the bony part above the eye sockets).

A skeleton's ancestry, or race, can be hard to figure out. Anthropologists look for general markers for specific ethnic groups. Caucasians, for example, often have narrow faces and prominent chins. People of African descent usually have wide nasal openings. Those of Asian or American Indian background generally have prominent cheekbones.

To complete the biological profile, the victim's height is estimated. The estimate is based on measurements of the long bones, such as the femur. Different calculations are used depending on the person's sex and ancestry.

The biological profile can be used to narrow down the possible identity of the victim. If police come up with the name of a possible victim, anthropologists can compare the characteristics of the remains with what is known of the alleged victim. They might compare **antemortem** and

Righting Wrongs

Forensic anthropologists are often called upon to investigate human rights violations and war crimes. Such work has carried forensic anthropologists to Iraq, Argentina, Rwanda, Guatemala, Bosnia, and many other locations. Often, anthropologists are called in when genocide has left mass graves full of hundreds of unidentified bodies. The bones in such graves are often mixed together. It can be difficult for anthropologists to even determine how many victims there are. Often, medical and dental records are not available to establish a positive identity. Anthropologists look for clues in the items—such as clothing—found in the grave. They also try to determine the cause of death. Identifying victims of atrocities is rewarding work. But it comes with its share of hazards, including death threats and unexploded land mines.

postmortem X-rays, for example. When someone breaks a bone in life, new bone grows over the break to repair it. This leaves a scar unique to that person. That scar can still be seen in the bone after death. If the scar matches the earlier X-rays, it confirms the identity.

Forensic anthropologists are sometimes also able to help the pathologist pinpoint the cause of death. A break to a small bone in the upper throat, called the hyoid, can mean that a person was strangled, for example. Bullet and knife wounds also leave distinctive marks on bone.

In one case, a decomposed corpse was found in the basement of a house. Injuries to the bone indicated that the man had been both stabbed with a knife and shot with a shotgun. Confronted with the evidence, his wife and stepdaughter confessed to the killing.

Forensic anthropologists often work with forensic odontologists, or dentists. Teeth are even stronger than bone. They are sometimes all that remains of the victim of a fire or explosion. Like bones, teeth can be used to establish age. A young child's teeth fall out and are replaced by adult teeth in a specific order. In addition, adult teeth show signs of wear that can help indicate age.

Detailed dental records exist for most people in the U.S. These records include X-rays and information on dental abnormalities and procedures. It is highly unlikely that any two people would have exactly the same teeth and dental work. This means that dental records can be used to establish a definitive identity. After a tsunami devastated much of the Southeast Asian coastlines in 2004, dentists from around the world sent dental records of patients who were known to be missing. Dentists were able to use these records to identify many remains. For those who didn't have records, the dentists often used photos of the victims smiling.

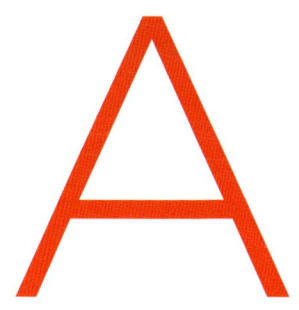

A skull and teeth cannot give a picture of what a person looked like in life. But sometimes a

MEDICAL EXAMINATION

OPPOSITE Facial recognition is widely used to help identify the remains of unknown individuals. Sculpted facial reconstructions can be scanned into the Federal Bureau of Investigation's Next Generation Identification (NGI) database to make use of its facial recognition software.

picture is exactly what's needed to identify a victim. So forensic artists may be asked to reconstruct a person's face. Sometimes, forensic artists sketch a two-dimensional picture of the face. Other times, they layer clay over the skull to create a three-dimensional replica. Facial reconstructions are often done by computer as well. This can help generate many possibilities in a short amount of time. "We have to guesstimate some features," according to forensic anthropologist Wally Schier. "And the computer modeling allows us to make a dozen faces with all the variations possible for that skull. It also lets us play with skin tone or hair color, things we can't know for certain." If someone recognizes the computer-generated image, the computer can compare photographs of the missing person with the model. This might prove an exact match. Or it might rule out the person as the victim.

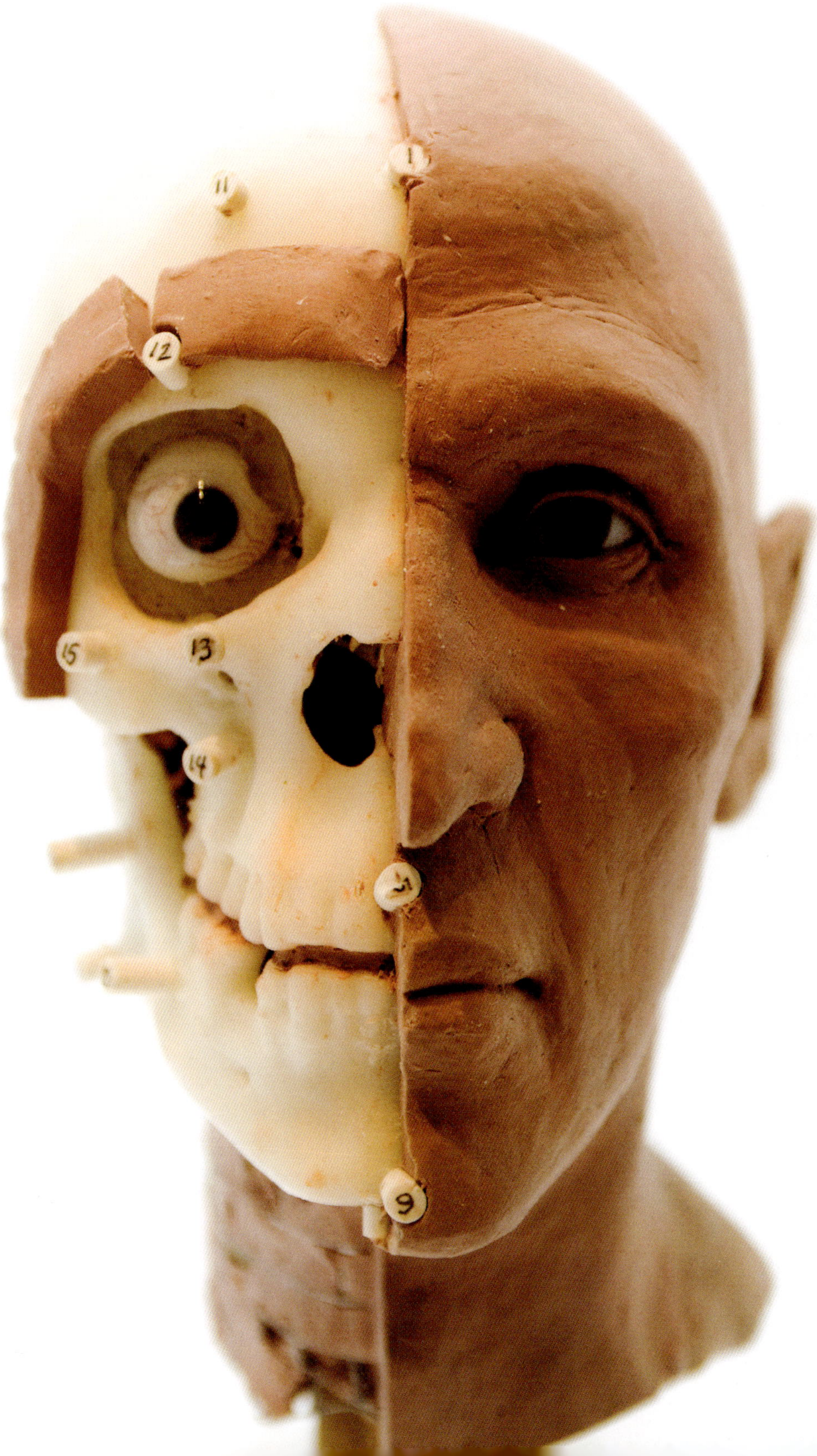
11
1
12
15
13
14
9

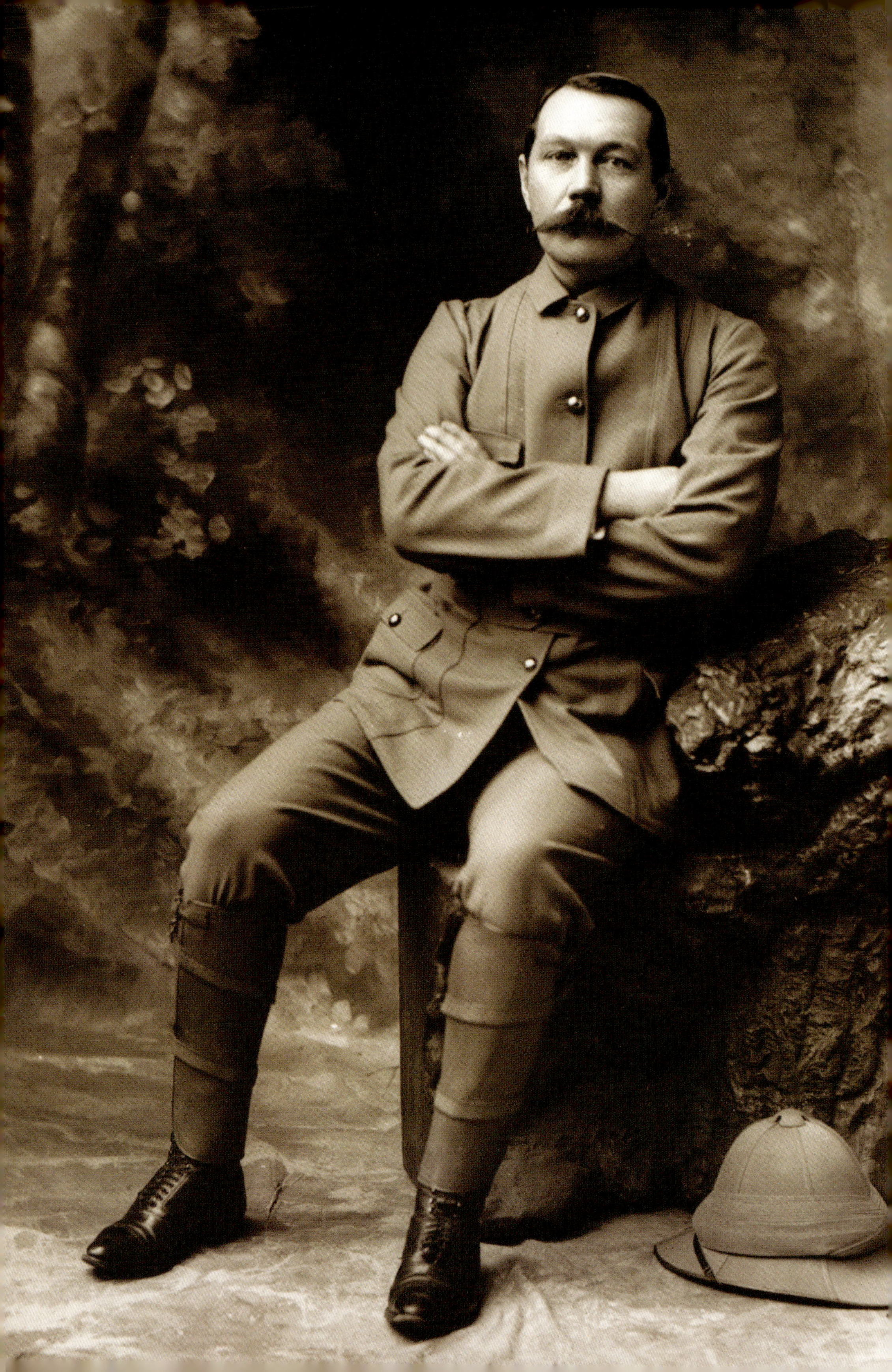

MEDICAL EXAMINATION

Fictional Forensics

Perhaps the most famous fictional detective of all time, Sherlock Holmes was no stranger to the scientific examination of dead bodies. The creation of Scottish author Sir Arthur Conan Doyle, Holmes was based on forensics expert Joseph Bell, a medical professor at the University of Edinburgh. Bell **dissected** corpses to teach medical students about the human body. Holmes, too, is said to have spent plenty of time in dissecting

OPPOSITE: Sir Arthur Conan Doyle's fictional detective began using forensic science to identify causes of death, as well as suspects, even before many police departments implemented such practices.

51

rooms studying bodies. In *A Study in Scarlet* (1887), readers learn that Holmes sometimes beats dead bodies with a stick. His purpose is "to verify how far bruises may be produced after death."

Today, forensic fiction is more popular than ever, both in print and on the screen. Many bestselling novels feature forensic pathologists and anthropologists. Like Holmes, these characters are often based on real-life experts. And many of them are written by people who know the field because they've been part of it. Author

Patricia Cornwell, for example, based her tough-as-nails medical examiner Kay Scarpetta on Marcella Fierro, former chief medical examiner for Virginia. Before writing crime novels, Cornwell worked as a technical writer and computer analyst in the Virginia medical examiner's office.

Forensic anthropologist Kathy Reichs has also turned her expertise to writing fiction. Her books about forensic anthropologist Temperance Brennan inspired the television program *Bones*. Reichs, who is a professor of anthropology at the University of North Carolina, said she turned to fiction to bring "my science to a broader audience."

Dozens of television crime shows feature forensic investigators using science to solve their cases. The first TV series with a forensic pathologist in the starring role

OPPOSITE Although television shows such as *CSI: NY* may be based on real-life events and examiners, much of the technology and equipment shown would be out of reach for the average medical examiner's office and its tight budget.

was *Quincy, M.E.* The show aired from 1976 to 1983. In recent years, pathologists have played key roles on shows such as *CSI: Crime Scene Investigation*, *NCIS*, *Law & Order*, *Crossing Jordan*, and *Body of Proof*.

Many of these shows have a foundation in real life. The coroner's office in Clark County, Nevada, for example, served as the model for *CSI*. Sometimes crime shows even take inspiration from real-life cases. For instance, one episode of *Crossing Jordan* was based on a real-life case in which lividity played a key role. The lividity pattern on a body dumped on the side of the road showed an imprint of the killer's license plate, which had been stored in his trunk with the body. The imprint led police right to the killer.

Of course, not everything about forensic fiction is true to life. For one thing, there are more autopsies per-

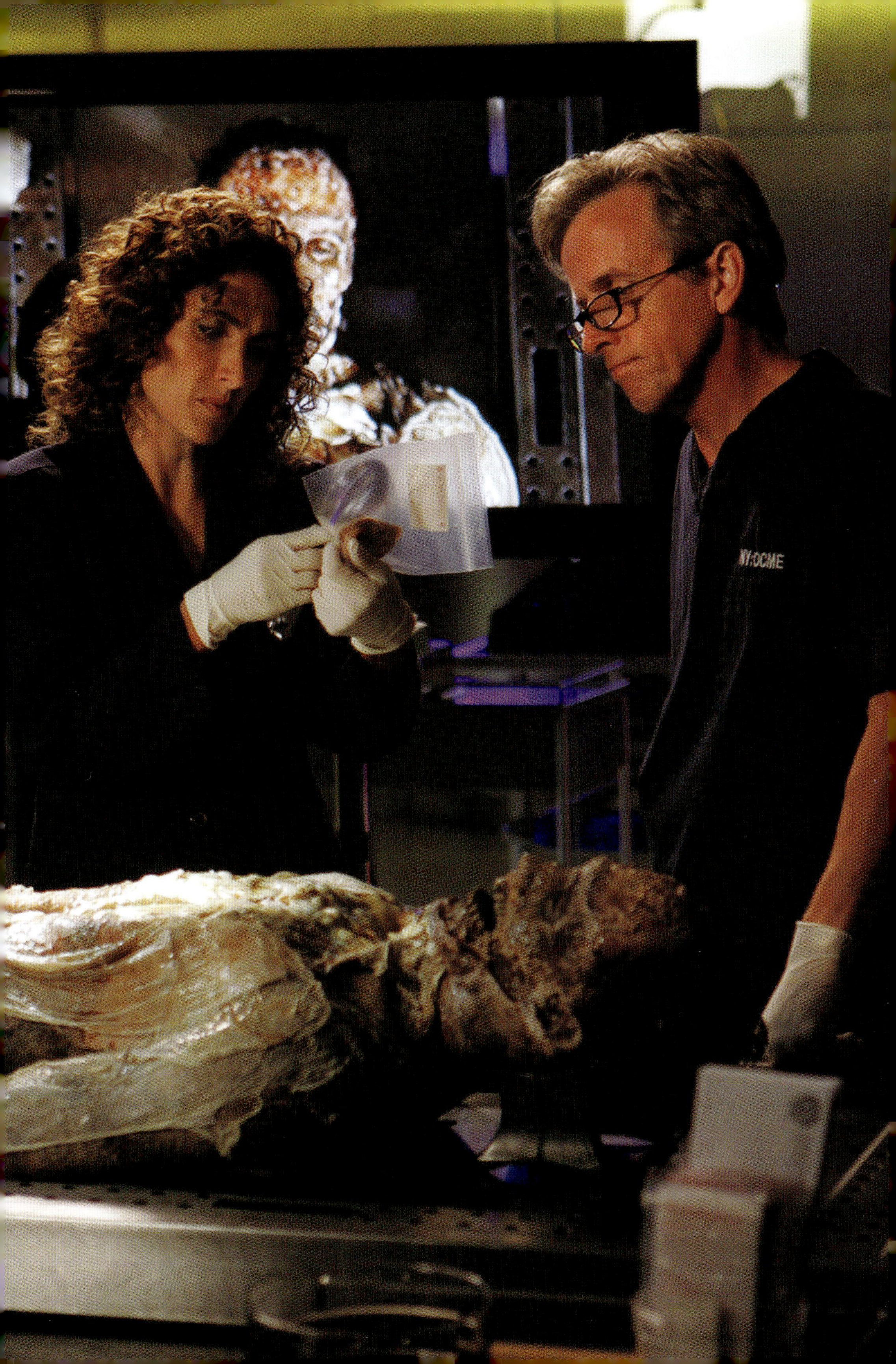
NY:OCME

formed on TV than in real life. In reality, many states have cut back on autopsies to save money. In addition, fictional forensic scientists usually have much nicer labs and equipment than those in real life. "Watch an episode of *CSI* and you would think forensic investigators move in a world of lab coats fresh from the cleaners ... and autopsy tables artfully—and pointlessly—underlit in purple," said journalist Jeffrey Kluger. According to Reichs, "Most crime labs can't afford what you see on TV." In some cases, medical examiners don't even have adequate lighting or access to refrigerated storage for the bodies they need to examine. And no real-life medical examiner would show up to examine a crime scene in an expensive suit and heels. "This job smells; it's dangerous, and you have to be really careful," said medical examiner Michael McGee. "The characters on TV never talk about bodies that are positive for hepatitis or HIV."

In addition, while many of the methods used in crime fiction are based on real life, they might go beyond what is really possible. "Sometimes a technique may have some legitimacy to it," Reichs said, "but it's pushed way beyond where it ought to be used." On *Quincy*, for example, the medical examiner could place the time of death to within a few minutes—rather than the several-hour time frame that can realistically be determined.

Probably the biggest difference between real life and fiction is that real examiners never take on the role of detective. But in fiction, this happens all the time. *Bones'* Temperance Brennan, for instance, often joins her partner, FBI agent Seeley Booth, in questioning witnesses and interrogating suspects. Unlike her character, Reichs says, "I work with the detectives, but I don't go and meet with families or interview suspects." In some cases, fictional forensic experts even come head-to-head with the bad guys. In Cornwell's novel *The Body Farm* (1994), for example, Kay Scarpetta faces off with a murderer, whom she kills with a shotgun.

Of course, novels and television shows aren't always trying to be accurate. They also have to consider entertainment value. "We start with reality and we deviate from there," said Donna Cline, a technical adviser for *Bones*. But some in the legal community fear

BELOW The TV show *Bones* is a dramatization of forensic anthropologist Kathy Reichs's experiences, supplementing the facts of daily life with exciting fictional details to attract viewers. *Bones* aired from 2005 through early 2017.

MEDICAL EXAMINATION

TAKEAWAY

"Medical examiners must deal with the increasingly unrealistic expectations of the public to have exact and immediate answers."

that deviation from reality may confuse readers and viewers. And those readers and viewers may one day serve as jurors.

Since 2002, debate has raged over whether forensic fiction creates a phenomenon known as the "*CSI* Effect," leading jurors to have unrealistic expectations of what forensic science can do. "Medical examiners must deal with the increasingly unrealistic expectations of the public to have exact and immediate answers," said John Howard, former president of the National Association of Medical Examiners (NAME). Coroner Mike Murphy agreed, saying that the shows lead people to believe "that we're supposed to solve a crime in 60 minutes with 3 commercials. It doesn't happen that way."

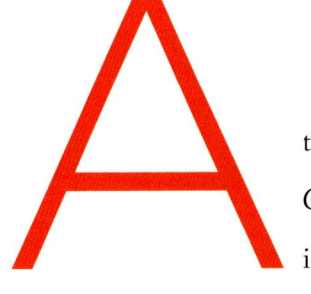

At the same time, Murphy said the *CSI* Effect has had a positive impact as well. "It has brought what we do from the shadows—where people really didn't want to know and didn't care what we do—to the bright light of day," he said. Anthony Zuiker, creator of *CSI*, said his goal for the show was to make a difference in real-life crime solving. "We hoped that the show would raise awareness and get more funding into crime labs so people felt safe in their communities," he said. "And we're still hoping that the government will catch up."

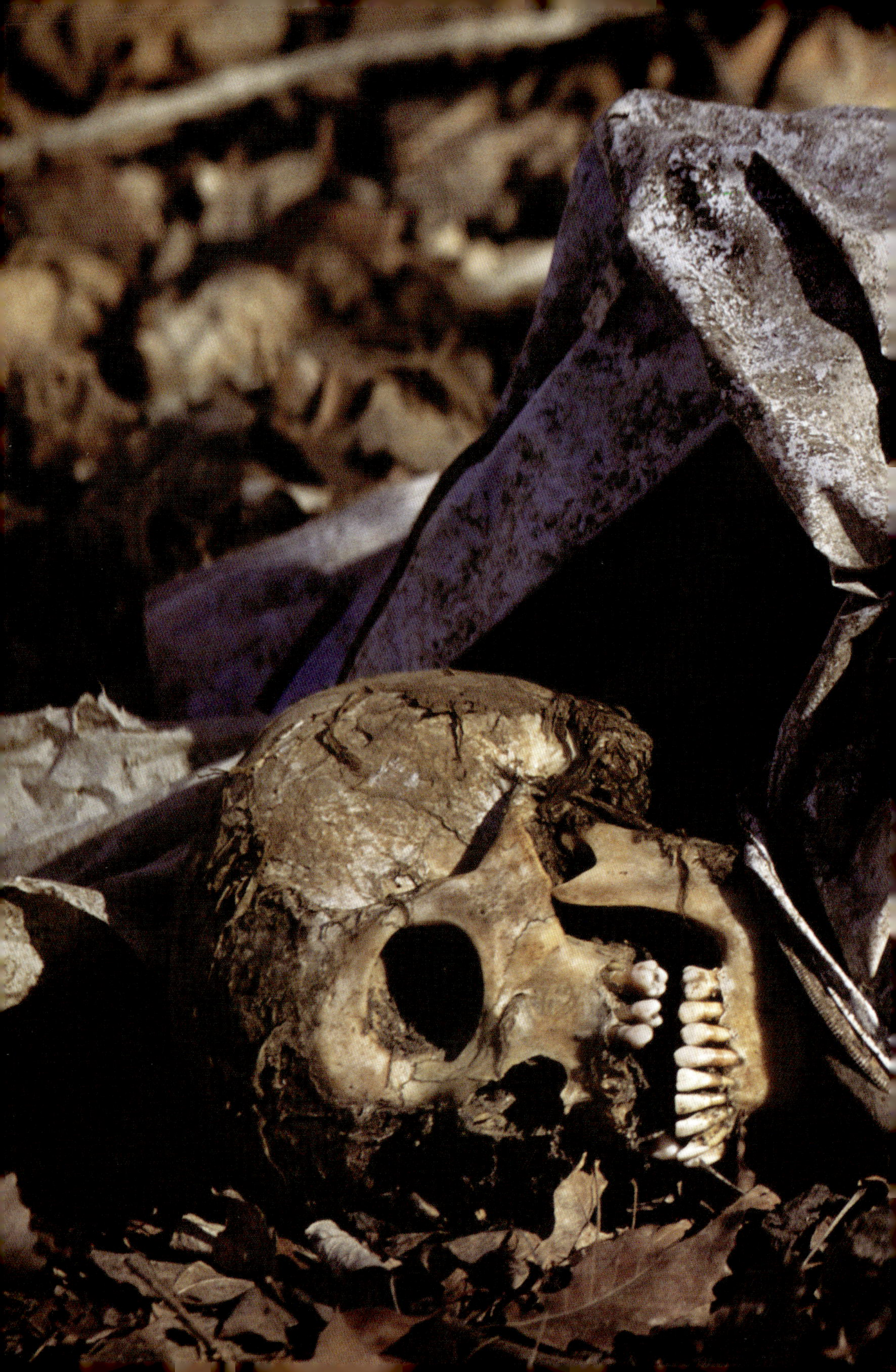

The Body Farm

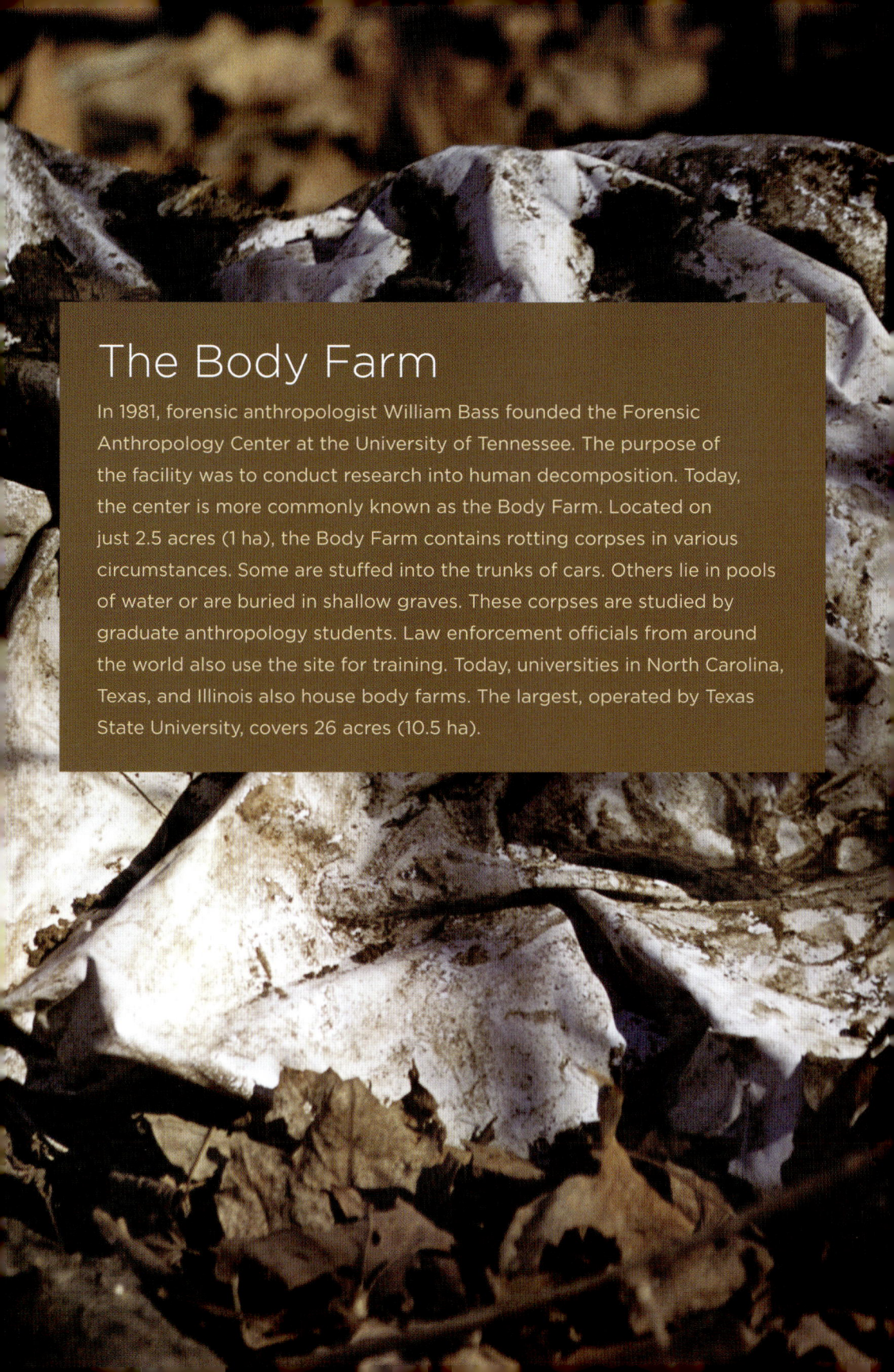

In 1981, forensic anthropologist William Bass founded the Forensic Anthropology Center at the University of Tennessee. The purpose of the facility was to conduct research into human decomposition. Today, the center is more commonly known as the Body Farm. Located on just 2.5 acres (1 ha), the Body Farm contains rotting corpses in various circumstances. Some are stuffed into the trunks of cars. Others lie in pools of water or are buried in shallow graves. These corpses are studied by graduate anthropology students. Law enforcement officials from around the world also use the site for training. Today, universities in North Carolina, Texas, and Illinois also house body farms. The largest, operated by Texas State University, covers 26 acres (10.5 ha).

MEDICAL EXAMINATION

Last Chance

Another result of the *CSI* Effect is that jobs in forensic science are more popular than ever. But careers in forensic pathology, anthropology, and odontology require lengthy training. Forensic pathologists, for example, must attain a medical degree. Then they spend four years in a pathology **residency**, followed by another one to two years in forensic pathology training. Forensic anthropologists generally spend 6 to 10 years earning a master's degree or **doctorate** in anthropology. And odontologists attend dental school. Afterward, they enroll in an additional two- to five-year program in forensic odontology.

Most forensic pathologists are employed by the city, county, or state medical examiner or coroner's office. Others work for hospitals, universities, or private consulting firms. Some larger medical examiner's offices employ full-time forensic anthropologists and odontologists. But most anthropologists are employed by museums and universities. They consult with law enforcement only as necessary. Forensic odontologists may also be employed by law enforcement agencies, law firms, or insurance companies.

Forensic specialists need strong speaking skills to present their findings in court. They should also be able to handle gruesome sights. In addition, they must be prepared to attend the scene of a crime at any time of the day or night. There are health risks involved, too, as corpses may carry diseases and viruses such as HIV.

In addition to helping solve crimes, forensic pathologists also play a preventive role. Through autopsies, they might become aware of a contagious disease, environmental hazard, or other public health threat. In 2001, for example, medical examiners alerted authorities of anthrax attacks against political and media figures. Autopsies can also help identify workplace hazards or

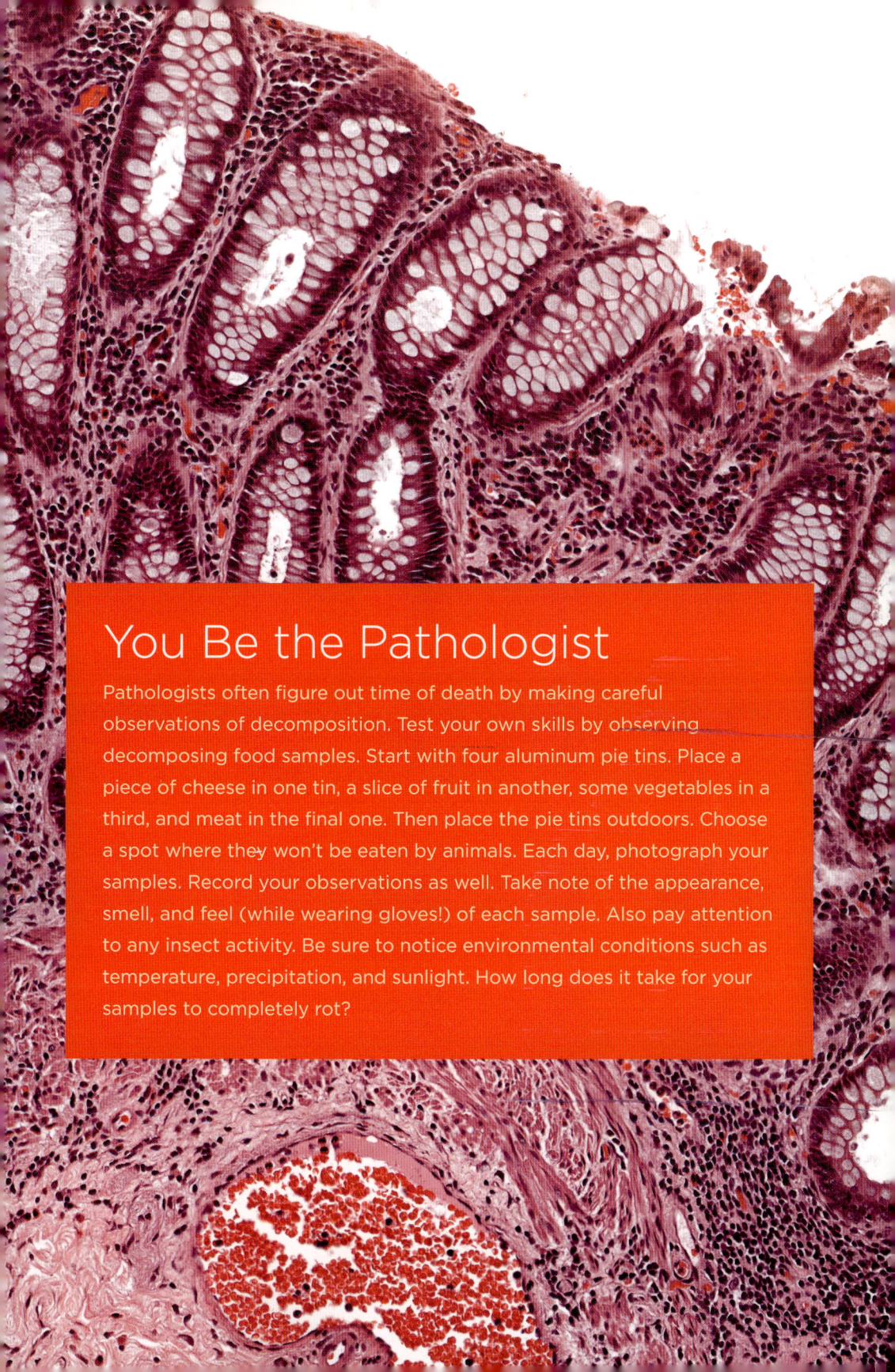

You Be the Pathologist

Pathologists often figure out time of death by making careful observations of decomposition. Test your own skills by observing decomposing food samples. Start with four aluminum pie tins. Place a piece of cheese in one tin, a slice of fruit in another, some vegetables in a third, and meat in the final one. Then place the pie tins outdoors. Choose a spot where they won't be eaten by animals. Each day, photograph your samples. Record your observations as well. Take note of the appearance, smell, and feel (while wearing gloves!) of each sample. Also pay attention to any insect activity. Be sure to notice environmental conditions such as temperature, precipitation, and sunlight. How long does it take for your samples to completely rot?

dangers in vehicle designs. They can even help spot the work of serial killers by noting a series of murders carried out using the same methods. On a more personal level, medical examiners might discover a **genetic** disorder in the deceased. This could prompt family members to seek testing and possible treatment for the same disorder.

Despite these positives, the death investigation system in the U.S. is not without problems. One of the biggest issues is a lack of funding. This has resulted in a decline in the number of autopsies performed. In many states, it has become routine not to autopsy suicides or car accidents. Elsewhere, no one over the age of 60 is autopsied, unless they were obviously the victim of a violent death. In Oklahoma, the cutoff age is 40. But many pathologists worry that such policies make it easy to miss murders.

Some experts also take issue with the way the death investigation system in the U.S. is set up. A 2009 report by the National Academy of Sciences (NAS) criticized many aspects of forensic science. It was particularly severe regarding the dual coroner/medical examiner system. The report pointed out that coroners do not need to have any qualifications. In one county, a 17-year-old high school senior was chosen as deputy coroner. The dual system also means that there are no national standards or oversight for death investigators.

Such a lack of standards has led to many mistakes. In Massachusetts, for example, the medical examiner's office reportedly lost body parts. In Michigan, an autopsy of a man pulled from a lake failed to note the bullet wound in his neck. In some offices, board certification is not a requirement for employment. So even pathologists who failed their board exams can be hired.

Some medical examiners and coroners have also been accused of showing bias. Most medical examiners and coroners work for the government. They are often considered to be on the same "team" as the police and prosecutors. This means that they might feel pressured to help secure a conviction. "The cops say, 'Hey, if you can place the time of death at 3 A.M., we've got this guy cold. After that he's got an alibi,'" Michael Baden says. "And then you start hearing about all the hideous things the 'bad guy' has supposedly done." But, Baden points out, "You must always ally yourself only with the science.... Sometimes, of course, the cops have got it wrong."

To strengthen forensic science in the U.S., the NAS report suggested taking several drastic steps. One was eliminating the coroner system (a recommendation first made in 1928). Other recommendations included making the medical examiner system separate from law enforcement. In addition, the NAS said that national standards should be set for medical examiners' offices.

And board certification should be required for all forensic pathologists.

Even as they search for ways to correct problems in their field, forensic pathologists are also looking to the new technologies of the future. High-tech methods such as multidetector **computed tomography** (MDCT) can be used to scan victims' bodies. The scans provide views of both soft tissue and bones. The machine can even be used to detect brain injuries and drowning, evidence of which may be difficult to discover through traditional

BELOW Today, 3D printers can be used to print skull replicas from scans. Printed copies of the skull can then be used in facial reconstructions and in comparing photographs of missing persons.

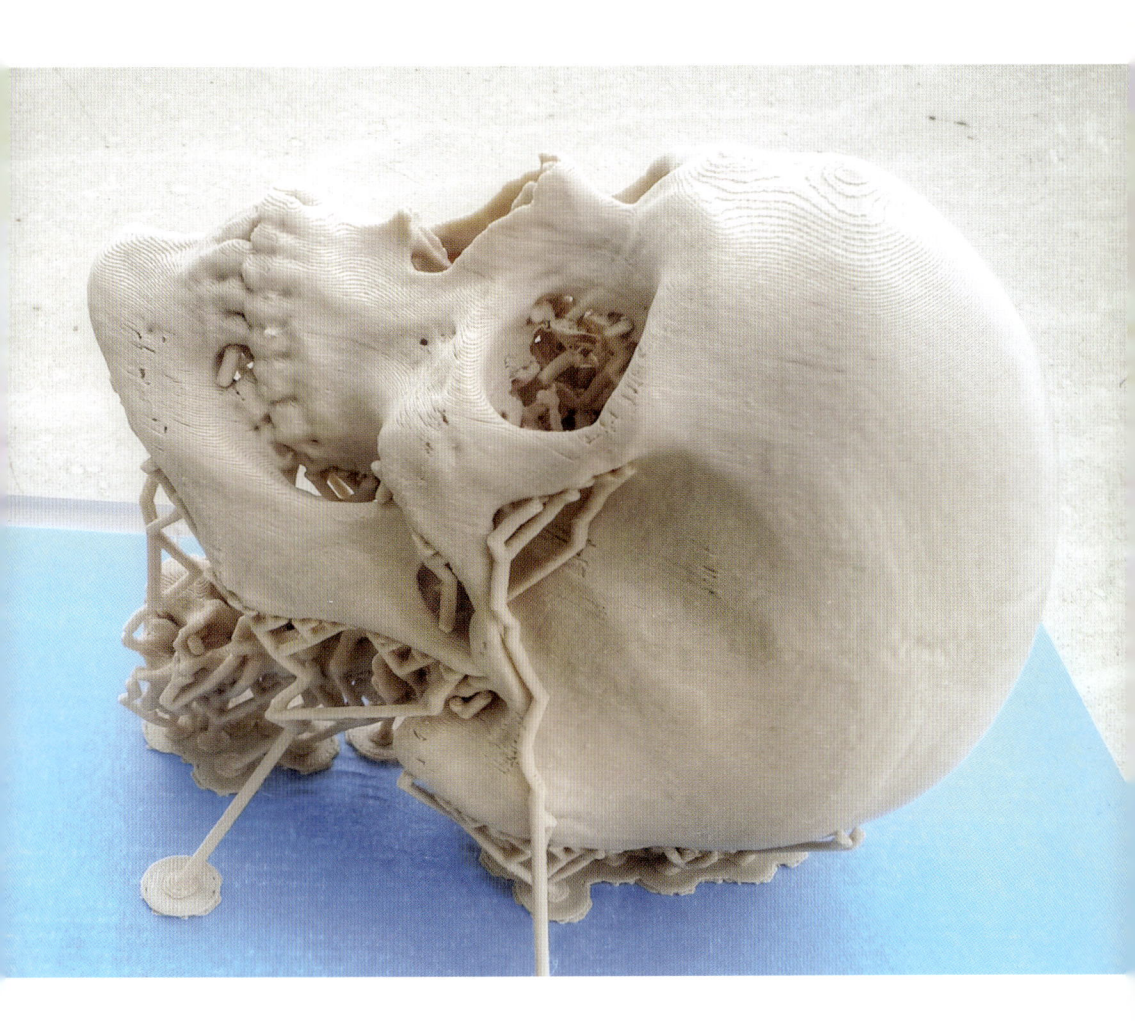

MEDICAL EXAMINATION

autopsies.

The Institute of Forensic Medicine at the University of Zurich in Switzerland is also working on a virtual autopsy technique called "virtopsy." A virtopsy uses CT scans and **magnetic resonance imaging** (MRI) to provide a three-dimensional internal view of the body. A robotic system known as a virtobot can also be used to take samples from the corpse. According to Michael Thali, director of the Institute, the virtopsy can identify "60 percent to 80 percent of the forensic causes of death. In the future, that will change the world in forensics." Since a virtopsy is much faster than a traditional autopsy, some experts hope its widespread use could allow for more bodies to be autopsied.

Ultimately, a forensic examination is the last chance for the victim of a crime to tell his or her story. As author

Patricia Cornwell put it, "The dead have much to say that only people with special training and special gifts have the patience to hear." Those people are forensic pathologists, anthropologists, and odontologists. What the dead tell them might reveal how the person died. And, if it was the result of a crime, it might even help catch the person responsible.

Glossary

anatomical	related to the structure of living things
antemortem	occurring before death
asphyxiation	to kill someone by cutting off their oxygen supply, such as through suffocating or smothering
bile	a bitter, yellow-brown fluid secreted by the liver to aid in digestion
coagulates	clots and forms a soft, semisolid mass
computed tomography	an imaging device that uses computers and X-rays to create a three-dimensional image of body structures
dissected	cut apart or separated a body to study or examine it
DNA	abbreviation for deoxyribonucleic acid, a substance found in the cells that contains genetic information that determines a person's characteristics, such as eye color
doctorate	the highest degree given by a university
enzymes	proteins that can start or speed up a chemical reaction
genetic	having to do with genes, which transfer traits from a parent to a child

hypothermia	a condition in which a person's body temperature drops too low, which can lead to death
magnetic resonance imaging	a technique that uses a strong magnetic field to produce computerized images of internal tissues
pathogens	things that can cause a disease, including viruses and bacteria
plague	a highly contagious, widespread disease that causes high numbers of deaths
postmortem	occurring after death
residency	a period of advanced medical training carried out within a hospital
toxicological	related to the study of poisons
trace evidence	tiny pieces of evidence, often too small to be seen by the naked eye, that can serve to identify an individual or connect the individual to a specific location
tuberculosis	a contagious disease that affects the lungs
vitreous humor	the clear gel that fills the eyeball and doesn't decompose after death

Selected Bibliography

Baden, Michael, and Marion Roach. *Dead Reckoning: The New Science of Catching Killers*. New York: Simon & Schuster, 2001.

Committee on Identifying the Needs of the Forensic Sciences Community, National Research Council. *Strengthening Forensic Science in the United States: A Path Forward*. Washington, D.C.: National Academies Press, 2009. https://www.ncjrs.gov/pdffiles1/nij/grants/228091.pdf.

Dale, W. Mark, and Wendy S. Becker. *The Crime Scene: How Forensic Science Works*. New York: Kaplan, 2007.

Ferllini, Roxana. *Silent Witness: How Forensic Anthropology is Used to Solve the World's Toughest Crimes*. 2nd ed. Buffalo, N.Y.: Firefly Books, 2012.

Fisher, Barry A. J. *Techniques of Crime Scene Investigation*. 7th ed. Boca Raton, Fla.: CRC Press, 2004.

Genge, N. E. *The Forensic Casebook: The Science of Crime Scene Investigation*. New York: Ballantine, 2002.

Houck, Max M. *Forensic Science: Modern Methods of Solving Crime*. Westport, Conn.: Praeger, 2007.

Ricciuti, Edward. *Science 101: Forensics*. New York: HarperCollins, 2007.

Websites

CSI: The Experience Web Adventures
http://forensics.rice.edu/

Try your hand as a forensic pathologist through interactive games and training sessions.

PBS Nature: Crime Scene Creatures
*http://www.pbs.org/wnet/nature/crime-scene-creatures
-interactive-determine-the-time-of-death/4390/*

Test your forensic entomology skills by collecting insects from a body to figure out how long it has been dead.

Note: Every effort has been made to ensure that any websites listed above were active at the time of publication. However, because of the nature of the Internet, it is impossible to guarantee that these sites will remain active indefinitely or that their contents will not be altered.

Index

Antistius 31
autopsies 11, 12, 13, 21, 25, 26, 27-28, 31-34, 37, 38, 51, 54, 56, 66, 68-69, 70, 72, 74
  virtopsies 74
Barth, Debra 33
body farms 63
causes of death 10, 11, 12-13, 14, 25, 26, 31, 33-34, 39, 44, 45, 46, 72, 74, 75
Cornwell, Patricia 53, 58, 75
coroners 12, 13, 60-61, 65, 69, 70, 71
  Murphy, Mike 60-61
CSI Effect 60-61, 64
dangers 27, 44, 56-57, 66
decomposition 13, 18, 19, 21, 38, 39, 44, 46, 63, 67
Doyle, Sir Arthur Conan 51-52
  and Sherlock Holmes character 51-52
forensic anthropologists 10, 39-40, 42-43, 44, 45, 46, 48, 52, 53, 56, 57-58, 63, 64-65, 75
  Bass, William 63
  Reichs, Kathy 53, 56, 57-58
  Schier, Wally 48
forensic entomologists 19
forensic odontologists 10, 44, 46-47, 64, 65, 75
forensic pathologists 12-13, 27-28, 31, 32-34, 37, 45, 52, 64, 65, 66, 67, 69, 70, 72, 75
Institute of Forensic Medicine 74
law enforcement officials 10, 28, 43, 63, 65, 70, 71
legal proceedings 10, 37, 58, 60, 65, 70
manners of death 25, 26, 31-32, 33-34, 37, 44, 45-46, 68, 69
mechanisms of death 25-26
medical examiners 10, 12, 13-14, 17, 18, 21, 27-28, 53, 56-57, 60, 65-66, 68, 69, 70-71
  Baden, Michael 27-28, 70-71
  Fierro, Marcella 53

McGee, Michael 56-57
morgues 21, 27, 56
National Academy of Sciences (NAS) 69, 71-72
National Association of Medical Examiners (NAME) 60
  Howard, John 60
postmortem interval 14, 16-18, 19
  algor mortis 14, 16, 18
  livor mortis 16-17, 18
  rigor mortis 17-18
Song Ci 31
technologies 28, 45, 46, 72, 74
television 27, 53-54, 56-58, 60-61
time of death 14, 16-18, 19, 21, 57, 67
tools and equipment 27-28, 39, 56
victim identification 10, 28, 32, 39, 40, 42-43, 44, 45, 46-48
  biological profiles 40, 42-43, 44, 45
  dental records 44, 46-47
  facial reconstructions 48
Virchow, Rudolf 31